REFLECTIONS

REFLECTIONS

mirror of my mind

Omar H. Malik

authorHOUSE®

AuthorHouse™ UK Ltd.
1663 Liberty Drive
Bloomington, IN 47403 USA
www.authorhouse.co.uk
Phone: 0800.197.4150

Published by AuthorHouse   01/21/2014

ISBN: 978-1-4918-9192-6 (sc)
ISBN: 978-1-4918-9209-1 (e)

Contents

I dedicate this book to my dearest wife Martina
and my two daughters Tina and Roma.

POETRY IN MOTION

An expression of emotion,
Of words in animation,
A philosophical message,
An allegorical passage,
An observation captured,
In lucid language pictured,
An enlightened literature,
A chronology of culture,
A reflection of life and time,
Expressed in rhythm and rhyme.

22.12.2013

A MOMENT TO CHERISH

A star spangled warm summer's night,
Full moon, not a hint of cloud in sight,
My heart feels happy and content,
Let this be a rare motionless moment!

My love of life close beside me,
The most beautiful sight I live to see,
Stars twinkling in the night sky,
I see reflection in her sparkling eye.

A moment to treasure and cherish,
Time dare not attempt to perish!
Oh no, this visual sensory and vivid imagery
I will capture it in my inner core of memory.

Moments time doesn't allow us to borrow,
Moments of happiness or moments of sorrow,
One solitary entrance then the final exit,
Time's never meant to turn back and revisit.

An eternal journey of wondrous hollow,
Footsteps only memories can cherish and follow.
So, let me cherish this enchanting moment
For the present and for memories content.

In the deep of dark, yet, sparkling night,
A breathtaking illuminating compelling sight,
Enchanting, echoing, gazing sky bound,
I experience a sensation of music without sound.

June 2013

AUTUMN LEAVES

On a sunny Autumn's day,
Walking in the park aimlessly,
Watching children happily at play,
Then I looked up and saw suddenly,
A leaf from a maple tree falling,
Dancing, dropping, smiling at me,
Wavering, quavering, calling, calling
And floating over a gentle breeze, I see,
Golden colours, mild sun kissed,
Beckons others to join and play.
A touch to senses, glad I hadn't missed;
On floor many more leaves gather and lay.

Falling leaves' one last dance
Of the final hours,
Autumn weaves carpets
Of many mixed colours.
Bare boughs, though, wailing
Anticipating freezing frost
And winter's naked dwelling
As the leaves, finally, are lost.

10. 11.2011

A THOUGHT FOR LIFE

When you are young and simple,
Everyone loves your smile and dimple.
When young, you long to grow old,
Every day you discover things untold.
Things you love and things you hate,
You struggle through life to defy your fate.
One day, alas! You do grow old and wonder,
Isn't life short? And there is no time to ponder!

21.5.1989

A RIVER'S TALE

I rise from a crystal clear spring
In trickles and trickles and tickled, I sing
And dance down in an echoing sound,
Dashing, daringly, for the lower ground.

Dizzy fall mountain high, fearless, intrepid,
Gathering white-water down a rapid,
Negotiating wild, deep, rocky gorge
For miles and miles and miles ahead I forge.

Now at a gentle pace, through lush lowland plains,
Valleys of green vegetations and cultivated grains,
Dividing bustling villages, markets, towns and cities,
I visit many countries of diverse nationalities.

Fish and amphibians keep me in constant company,
Birds sing and accompany all through my journey,
I meet and greet rills, brooks and other tributaries,
Fishermen dropping nets, sailing boats and ferries.

I reflect at shinning sunrise, shimmering sunset,
And deep blue sky until dark rain clouds beset,
Floating white clouds happily wave as they pass by,
I see moon smiling, stars sparkling in a clear night sky.

I see lovers, linking hands, walking on promenades,
Beside buildings of admirable architectural facades.
In stride, rushing under many manmade beautiful bridges,
Interacting reflecting lights and shades of lonely ridges.

I am a free flowing river, lifeline of many civilizations,
Sourcing food, water and forms of transportations.
Sadly, in too much rain I swell and flood and I destroy
And in drought I fail to contribute 'cause I am dry.

I witnessed lands on my bank growing grains or grazing,
Open parks and playing fields turned into housing,
Brutal battles fought fearlessly at nations' call
Mighty civilizations rise in glory, then fall.

Rowing boats, sailing boats, steam boats, motor boats,
On my waters they ply.
Fishing boats, merchant boats, pleasure boats,
On my waters they rely.

On my long journey I negotiated many locks, weirs and
bends,
Now, in view, I see the estuary waves and here my journey
ends.
Tides are welcoming me and leading towards the deep sea
And the sea in turn soon deeper ocean bound be.

11.12.2013

A LOUT'S LEGACY

Call me a lout, if you will,
Life didn't offer me a fair deal.

A product of two people's reckless encounter—
Unwanted, unloved, into their tangled life I enter.
Bore many more children—different fathers,
State benefit fuels her appetite—poor single mother!

Often abused, her encounters beg to be discreet,
Leaves me no options but to seek refuge on the street.
When allowed in, I am in a tearful and tormented state;
I cry and cry, why have I, such a cruel fate?

Admit, there is a kind of roof over my head,
'Tis hardly a home—where love is dead!
What is love? Have I ever experienced it?
Is it any wonder, why in society I am a misfit?

Fate failed badly, not securing a loving childhood,
My cognitive sense starved of an appetite that is good.
A precious chapter lost, can't bring back or borrow.
Resort to narcotics, one option, to drown my sorrow!

'Somebody help me' I cry, in a state of convulsion;
Society's response resonate round, ruffled repulsion.
Thrown in a heap of unwanted—a term in a prison;
Is that a cure or filling my mind with more poison?

Having suffered already, a prolonged tragedy,
A term in jail, would seem a double jeopardy!
Resources better deployed, not building more jail,
But, efforts to deter and reform parents who fail.

Terms of fate and society proved equally cruel.
Give me a sense of purpose or affection to dwell.
Show me a little love, I may, learn to reciprocate.
Offer me not punishment, but guidance to defy my fate.

01.12.2011

A HOLY SANCTUARY?

What is the purpose of life? The eternal question.
Mystery shrouds the source and origin of creation.
A fragile, fallible life leading to a 'dead end' certainty,
Gave birth to a divine power, a revered merciful deity.
A hint of heaven, of eternity for a presumed everlasting soul,
Provides a purposeful, positive, proximity and
an achievable goal!

Life in many different guise, a constant struggle for most,
A gratifying sense—we are under gazing eyes of a gracious Host.
Faith features an orderly boundary, an escape and
luminous hope
For the daily struggle and survival, seems a fair oasis and scope.
For the fear of afterlife, infinity and unfathomed uncertainty
Religion resonates respite for the simple price of conformity.

Religion, historically state sponsored, faith and dogma dictated,
Nonconformists executed, persecuted or at best discriminated.
Forced indoctrination over time turned into tradition and culture,
War, trade and migration helped initiate a secular structure.
Science, based on knowledge, opened an intelligent debate,
Misconstrued religious teachings, as yet, failing to accommodate.

Beyond any reason, evidence denied, faith's impression is blind.
For a higher animal, with concept for reason,
an exceptional find!
If there is only one God we are expected to believe and obey,
Why are there so many religions and so differently we pray?
Believers in every religion, cast and society claiming propriety,
Each promising hope, sanctuary, closure and proximity.

A social animal, comfortable in a clan, club or a community
To secure the inherent sense of survival and sanctity.
For the shepherd a convenient campus for control with fear,
Undertaking assurances for the afterlife that may endear.
The privileged, thus, had the masses blinkered and schooled.
An easy nonconfrontational method, rulers devised and ruled.

Fundamental difference remains in religion's prophecy of
creation,
Opposed to Darwin's theory of evolution and natural selection.
A debate and disagreement about afterlife, equally, being
kept alive,
Yet, happily, continued progression in science is allowed to thrive.
Faith, mother of civilisation and culture, of music, arts and
literature;
Temples, pagodas, churches and mosques of towering
architecture.

In the context of faith many lives have been fulfilled,
In the defence of faith many more, sadly, have been killed.
Many, positively, sought purity of soul, peace and
enlightenment
Through religious faith and made a purposeful commitment.
An omnipotent, omnipresent, merciful, Creator religions
preach,
A life of injustice, suffering, cruelty and killing—a paradox
and a breach.

10.11.2012

A RIPE OLD AGE

At a ripe old age,
Removed from centre stage,
Lost all audience and fan,
Who wants to listen to
A grumpy old man?

Mind though, is alert and willing,
Body, may be, sagging and failing,
Moving slower and slower,
Confined in a restful bower.

Old values violated day by day,
Fake and virtual is here to stay,
Brand new wired phenomenon,
The old has no legs to stand on.

Medical science performed miracles,
Extended life-span, reduced wrinkles,
Helping to grow old gracefully,
Seeing through an old age cheerfully.

Some, on reflection, cheerful and content,
Others, in pain, fearful of afterlife event.
The fortunate leaves memories to be cherished,
The unfortunate, sadly, unceremoniously perished.

18.02.2013

A WOMAN OF BEAUTY

She is a rare beauty, divinely planned,
An impression carefully crafted by divine hand,
A happy, smiling face, radiant, so pure!
Reflecting a refined heart's simple inner core.

Refreshing, like an early morning sun shining,
Eyes expressive, sparkling, like two stars defining!
Rosy cheeks, mirror her warm heart's inner glow,
Measures of makeup brushes forbidden to flow.

Luscious lips, a colour that rivals a bright red cherry,
A musical voice of speech eloquent not oratory.
Sparkling white teeth outshines perfect pearls,
Free flowing fine silky hair, some delicate curls.

Velvet smooth skin, san make-up, pure and clean.
Elegance, intelligence and presence, a kind, rarely seen.
Calm and cool temperament of angelic nature,
Walks at an animated rhythm of dancing posture.

Measure of vital statistics of enviable proportion,
Behold! A besotting, bewitching sight in motion.
A potential power able to build or destroy,
Like Cleopatra, Queen of Sheba and Helen of Troy.

At the height of youth a rhythm of life inspire,
At the height of youth every man's desire.
At low ebb of life an undesirable truth, beware!
Time's cruel imprint robs youth and beauty bare.

20.12.2013

A WALK BY THE SEA

Walking by the sea with the woman I love most,
On the beaches of beautiful Studland Bay,
A pretty place by the South Dorset coast,
Joyful moments, memories bring back to-day.

Waves are still breaking at the rocks shore bound,
Caressed by the gentle warm southerly breeze,
Rushing in, then out, soaking the sand around
In endless bouts that never seem to cease.

Sun umbrellas up, some lazing, some reading it seems,
Children and adults alike, busy building sand castles,
Some enjoying on the water in boats of their dreams,
Some sailing, some on jet skis testing their muscles.

Ladies lounge or stroll in fancy bikinis and swimsuits,
Taking it all in, for protection, rubbing on sun cream,
The adventurous types seem to be in topless pursuits,
Vendors in brisk business selling drinks and ice cream.

Mobile phones, not idle, busy texting and photo calls,
Babies in bonnets, toddlers in sun hats, look cute and jolly,
The energetic and playful busy bouncing beach balls,
Others relaxing or taking a stroll enjoying an ice lolly.

Infectious fun, the natural pull of sun, sand and sea,
Gentle breeze, warm and welcoming in wide open space,
The serene blue waters that tend to set our minds free,
Loving to leave behind the daily grind and rat race.

Here, no ranks, no possessions, all equal, all at play,
Children and grownups alike, all happy and gay.
As the sun sinks at the edge of Studland Bay,
We end what was, once again, a memorable day.

09.05.2012

BEAUTIFUL LIFE

Beautiful life, though 'tis struggle for many,
Yet, no one ever wishes to die—hardly any.

Beautiful is youth, full of life's expectations,
Sweet dreams and creative imaginations.
Beautiful is a woman full of feminine charm
And a baby in a young mother's arm.

Beautiful, and look our best when we smile,
And the young bride walking down the aisle.
Beautiful is a kiss, so tender and touching;
No other expression is worthy of matching.

Beautiful is love, a feeling so deep and divine,
A life without it is like a day without sunshine.
Beautiful is truth, so pure and yet so simple;
Saints we are not, but nearly, if always truthful.

Beautiful is music that matches our mood,
Jolly or melancholy, make us feel good.
Beautiful is a mountain, standing high!
Looking over the horizon, kissing the blue sky.

Beautiful is, watching the morning sunrise,
For late risers, may be a pleasant surprise.
Beautiful, just as well, as the sun sets slow,
Giving way, to the twinkling stars and the moon glow.

Beautiful is, a rambling river and a lake so serene
And restless waves of a deep blue sea that keep rushing in.
Beautiful is, the endless horizon and the pale blue sky,
Watching the birds spread their wings and away they fly.

Beautiful even cold winter's pure white snow,
That in turn, followed by spring's flower show.
Beautiful is summer sunshine and summer flowers;
Watching autumn's falling leaves so full of colours!

Beautiful baby's sweet smile and moments of joy,
Innocent childhood, equally, for a girl or for a boy.
Beautiful, is a man and a woman and the family;
Grandpa and grandma make it ever so jolly.

Beautiful feeling is to come home sweet home;
Does it matter—a hut or a place under a dome?
Beautiful, even the wild beasts in their own right,
Watching them in the wild is a delightful sight.

Beautiful, is a feeling of duty diligently performed;
Peace of mind, having time and energy well transformed!
Beautiful is life and all natures living creations,
Demands compromise for peaceful cohabitations.

Sandhurst 21.05.1984

BIRD IN A CAGE

Little bird in a gilded cage,
In a home placed centre stage,
Struggle free life and bouncing,
Away from predators pouncing.

But, the little bird wants to fly,
In wide open blue sky,
Spreading her wing,
Happily, glide or swing

And dreaming —
Free, flying!

Even when storm clouds gather,
In her rain soaked feather,
Looking for food and grain
And all efforts seem in vain.

Building and crafting own nest
For safety, shelter and rest
From weather beaten state,
Then a quest for a mate!

Call of the wild beckons,
Taste of sweet freedom reckons,
Picking wild fruits and berries
Guarding against adversaries.

Little bird's plea—
'please set me free'!

13.09.2012

CELEBRATIONS

A birth,
A new life on earth,
A fruit of love, a bundle of joy!
May be a girl or may be a boy.
Family and friends gather to congratulate,
A beautiful cause to celebrate.

Coming of age,
A step outside the parental 'cage'
Not severing the unique bond,
Remaining forever fond.
A curtain opener for a generation,
A notable cause for celebration.

On the day of wedding,
Tears of joy shedding,
With a solemn marriage vow,
A declaration of love now,
A grand feast and occasion,
A loving cause for celebration.

The first job,
Don't let the competition rob.
Chance to prove earnings capability
In terms of ability, skills and creativity.
A starting point, full of expectation,
A worthy cause for celebration.

A high office,
Not meant for the novice.
Opportunity for a few with ability,
Result of hard work and capability,
Creating quite an impression!
A prized cause for celebration.

A windfall,
An unexpected call,
A life changing event,
May be luck or God sent.
New curtain raiser in action,
An exciting cause for celebration.

A religious call,
A set day for all,
Global religious traditions,
Conformed by generations,
Conjured commercial exploitation!
A holy cause for celebration.

Anniversaries,
Important days in diaries,
Of marriage and of birth,
For merriments and mirth,
A jolly, jolly, occasion,
A core cause for celebration!

A commercial call,
Consumers tempted to fall,
For Valentine's Day,
Mother's day, Father's day.
Even Christmas sidestepped religion,
Now a consumer led celebration!

The final call,
When the curtains fall,
Family and friends once again gather,
To bid final farewell together.
A sad but sober occasion,
A solemn cause for celebration.

31.01.2012

CELEBRITY

Media manipulated and manufactured,
Well crafted and cleverly structured,
A cult and a culture prosy,
A flight of future fantasy,
A well laden lavish argosy.

Under a blinding spell of spotlight
That's intended for impairing sight,
Lured by a changing fate,
In a hollow hedonistic state,
Leading up to fame's gate.

Promising profusion of wealth,
Fans made to pay by stealth,
Unable to spot media's mission,
Euphoria impaired their vision,
On a pedestal, celebrity in position.

In heightened merriment fans squeal,
Letting the world know how ecstatic they feel.
Blind—reality they can't see.
Incredibly, for life of a celebrity
Fans do hold the key!

21.05.2012

CENOTAPH

Soldiers are ordered not to reason why,
They are to obey orders to do or die.
For nation's need, they are objects of sacrifice;
At the battle they fall like a throw of dice.

Never to return, on the battle fields many die.
Mothers and widows, hearts broken, they cry
Holding young orphans in close comfort of bosom,
Bewildered, betrayed, heartstrings in spasm.

In nations honour, for politics and belligerent power play
The young and the innocents are forced to pay,
Heartache and hardship families made to bear.
Safe from horror scenes of war, do the leaders truly care?

In November at the cenotaph in thought and
In presence the nation gathers.

To show gratitude, honour and respect
And a silent prayer.

Nov 2011

CONUNDRUM

Questions are many in view,
Answers read very few,
Yet, preachers preach,
Teachers teach,
Truths breach.

Politicians proclaim
They have the answers,
But can't cross party line
And party line markers
Donors' pockets define.

Bosses claim
They are infallible,
Workers tame,
Can't blame,
Else jobs untenable!

Public propensity to fight
For their legal right,
Rights relate to responsibilities
And Freedom isn't free,
Bound by legalities.

For the learned,
Knowledge is bliss!
Known only a fraction
Of what knowledge is.
The ignorant insists,
What you don't know
You don't miss.!

04.01.2014

DEBT BUBBLE

Savings, a safe umbrella for rainy days;
Debt fails to provide shelter and betrays.

Debt bubble, responsible for present
Economic malaise

May have in store, far reaching prospects
Than that we appraise.

What is described a bubble, sooner or later,
Destined to burst!

Proved its sheer inability to quench our
Insatiable thirst.

Debt based, consumer led, greedy, wasteful
Economic society

Utterly failed to enrich our mind or alleviate
Our anxiety.

Over consumption, leaves the mother
Nature bare!

Waste, pollution and ravaging of nature—
Should we care?

A change, from the present position of needless
Selfish greed

Offers time to care, share and understanding
Each other's need.

Ushering a new era of modest living style
Welcoming austerity!

May nourish our soul—an enlightened route
To prosperity!

27.11.2011

EARTHLY TIME

Blessed with a body and a brain function,
A natural progression of reason and action,
Power of goodness and the positive,
Challenged by evil and the negative;

A constant conflicting balancing act,
Even nature refused to remain intact.
Calm, contributing and generously giving,
When enraged, challenging for living.

Time tends forever running ahead and away,
Unwilling to hold good times long a bay.
Dynamic, defiant and determined to change old for new,
Refusing to stay stale, searching what's next in view.

Life time, finite, action packed, birth till end;
Nature's law, humans not equipped to bend.
For every action a reaction is plausible,
Often though, veiled, not clearly visible.

Actions well intended are seeds that bear fruit,
Actions evil will remain barren, bare and brute.
Time measured and an earthly—treasured theme,
Looking beyond will seem an extravagant dream!

21.05.2012

Omar H. Malik

FACE OF MODERN CONSUMERISM

A girl in her precious teens, at height of her beauty!
She is hiding under a mask of make-up, what a pity!
Victim of commercial pressure and publicity,
Young girls, unaware, hiding natural beauty
Under a mask of heavy chemical shower
Like a debased beautiful blooming flower!
Unblemished silky smooth skin softly sigh,
Mother of beauty, horrified, can but cry.

Natural beauty begs to blossom but blotted
Under thick, heavy, make-up and clotted.
Revealing the face of modern consumerism.
Multinationals hold power beyond criticism,
Lure of profit and greed, indeed, awesome!
Beauty is banished, not allowed to blossom!
When fresh flower of youth on a face blooms and blushes,
Down with make-up and manipulators brushes!

31.10.2011

FLOWERS

A blend of air, earth, rain and sunshine,
A beauty to behold, words fail to define,
Spring air whispering life to all plants bare,
Spring sunshine's tender touch has its share.

Flowers begin to bud and bloom as Spring inspire,
Snowdrops in white, daffodils in yellow, tulips in red attire,
Cherry blossoms, camellias, magnolias, azaleas aplenty,
All robed in bright colour of blossomed beauty.

Flowering in the wild, nature's own love child,
Heathers in heathland and primroses in field,
Bluebells in woodlands whispering and gay,
Rhododendrons adorned by multicoloured spray.

Roses are regal in beauty and elegance,
Honeysuckle and Jasmine's purity of fragrance,
Lily of the valley and lilies in the pond,
To sunshine and showers all colours respond.

Flowers, a profusion of colours so pure,
Touched! Then blemished for sure.
Delicate petals and sweet scented fragrance,
An awakening sense and a touch of romance.

Smiling and dancing as the light wind blows,
Radiant when the summer sun glows,
Sun kissed, morning mist, drops of dew,
Bounteous beauty beckons love that's true.

Flowers for a bride—a bouquet for her wedding,
A bunch or a bouquet for a heart-warming greeting,
Lights and lifts heavy hearts that's feeling down,
Flowers, an object of adoration, never a frown.

Flowers in fields, gardens and trees,
Happily, hosting butterflies and bees.
Flowers bud, flowers bloom, and flowers wither away,
Until, Spring air whispers life again, one sunny day.

31.12.2013

FOLLOW THE MAN IN THE MIDDLE

Hey, diddle, diddle,
Follow the man in the middle,
The one with the fiddle,
Playing a happy tune,
A happy happy tune!

Mr. Greedy is riding high,
But, not happy, wants more,
Mr. Needy can but sigh!
Hand to mouth, fearful,
Nothing saved in store.

The man in the middle
Is very happy, it seems,
Riding steady on his saddle,
Balancing two extremes,
Holding on to his fiddle.

Hey, diddle, diddle,
Follow the man in the middle,
The one with the fiddle,
Playing a happy tune,
A happy happy tune!

14.02.2013

FORTIETH ANNIVERSARY

That day the sun never failed,
Floating clouds happily sailed,
Stars twinkle toed in and out,
The moon, when won her bout
With the cloud, smiled as well.
Day, I fell in love, in a magic spell!

You touched my tender heart,
I knew, from you, I could never part.
Now, forty years of marital bliss!
Feels as fresh as the very first kiss.

Forty years on,
Time played its part and moved on,
Many dreams fulfilled,
Some may have failed to yield.

Let us pause and reflect
And sweet memories recollect.
Let me hold your tender hands
Oh! Sweet one!
I still desire only yours
Or none.

19.09.2012

HOME

Home sweet home,
Not merely a roof over head,
Following a day's work,
A place to return and rest in bed.

A mansion or a castle,
For some, a shelter at best.
A castle or a cottage,
Lovers' shared desired nest.

A place to watch,
Loving children growing up happily.
As time passes by,
Parents, slowly, grow old gracefully.

For the powerful,
A signature of status and chivalry.
For the rich,
A display of wealth and social rivalry.

Architectural expression of,
Human creativity and beauty.
Some proudly preserved,
As national heritage and property.

A sense of security,
Blessing of a serene sanctuary.
But, a house is not a home, palace or a shack,
Home is where memories full and a pull to come back!

17.11.2011

LET THE LITTLE BIRD FLY

I saw a pretty little bird fly,
Gently gliding, not too high.
Then, I saw a man with a gun;
Killing to him seemed 'good fun'.

As he got ready for action,
I prayed for the little bird's protection.
Gunman aimed at my pretty little bird,
The gun roared with a bang, I heard.

I dreaded, surely, my little bird was dead!
To my delight! She flew away, instead.
I thanked heaven, indeed, I was very glad!
Killing a helpless little bird is, so so sad.

09.08.2010

MERRY CHRISTMAS

Merry Christmas, noel,
Santa Claus and jingle bell,
The holly and the ivy,
Baubles, tinsels, fairy lights
On Christmas tree,
Festive decorations,
Funful celebrations.

A kiss under the mistletoe
Happy, ho, ho, ho,
Time to look forward
To a gift or a card.
Be it fairy tale or folly,
It's funful and jolly.

May be a commercial finesse,
Yet warming many hearts in goodness,
Embracing family togetherness and ties,
Relishing turkey, trimmings and mince pies,
Pulling crackers of funny hats and silly jokes,
Exchanging presents, overindulgence stokes.

Holy church in congregation,
Sermons and carols in progression,
A traditional, holy, Christian fest.
The holy image, slowly, fading time's test,
Tradition, though, being kept alive,
Merry consumerism is here to thrive!

End of a calendar year, a date set
For the year passed, to reflect,
For time present to celebrate,
For time future to contemplate.

24.12.2013

OF GOOD AND EVIL

Two opposite forces dwell and dominate human souls,
Good—creative, life preserving and life enhancing.
Evil—degenerating, destructing and life threatening!
Visions balancing life's journey between the two poles.

At times veiled, hard to figure, good or bad, right or wrong.
Opinion varies, depending on knowledge and perception.
Configurating conflict on the strength of habit and
conception,
Religion, local culture, relativity and vested interest strong.

History speaks volumes about evils of war negating peace.
Lessons never learnt, memories fail, evil clouds good sense,
Devil's action stirs up again and again in guise of defence,
Developing killing machines, therefore, unlikely to cease.

Nature lending a hand sheltering life and keeping us fed;
Being a towering example, indeed of goodness in action,
At times overwhelms, with immense power of destruction!
When she decides to raise her uncompromising head.

Disparity in cognition debilitating reason to function.
Survival of the fittest, domination by the strongest,
Fuelled by greed, ambition and rivalry to the test,
Results in a perpetual power play and damnation.

Faceless, it seems, one without the other entity,
Religions portray them as the saint and the devil,
A positive and negative charge, to function and fulfil,
Refusing to compromise, yet live in close proximity.

Good or evil, yin or yang, liberal or orthodox,
The conflict of the dynamic duo thus remains integral.
Two basic ingredients compete, yet cultivate survival,
Demands an enlightened mind that sees through the paradox.

11.11.2012

OH DREAM!

Oh dream!
Come but not as a nightmare
Unless, you wish to scare,
In fear, then, I shall scream!

Oh dream!
If you are sweet and sublime,
I welcome you time after time.
Show me an everlasting beam!

Oh dream!
My dedicated day dream,
Powering my vision to survive,
Turning stale moments to revive!

11.12.2011

PEBBLES

On a sunny summers day, headed for Brighton beach,
A journey from home, an hour and a half to reach.
Arrived, I chose a spot to sit on the pebbles,
Settled down on a blanket with a picnic for nibbles.

Under a clear blue sky reflecting on calm sea,
Relaxing, looking around, reflecting, that's me.

I started picking up some pebbles to bring back
A collection as an interesting souvenir pack.

Pebbles are silent witness, if only, they could speak,
Would provide with many answers we seek.
Colours not bright, but soft mellow rustic shades,
Over many decades, weather beaten, colour fades.

Origins relate back to earth's hard rocky crust,
Shaped by time and waves' relentless thrust,
Each different, shapes formed by waves' power spell,
Each survived long journey and own story to tell.

Engrossed in my thoughts, meanwhile, time moved on
Looking up, saw the sun at the western horizon
Changing colours from yellow to orange and finally red,
Slowly, went down, giving an illusion, as if resting on sea bed.

12.04 2013

PENDULUM

Pendulum swings high and low,
Swings left, swings right, to and fro,
Tick tock, tick tock, counting time,
Sound of clock in a rhyme.

For time past, good memories cherished
And bad ones wish to be perished,
But, lessons are there to be learnt,
Books better bestowed not burnt.

Present's passage precious and brief,
Actions' measure deserved joy or grief,
Present, footing foundation for future,
Barring, unknown forfeiture or whims of nature.

Future phased out of sight,
Flame of hope, may throw some light!
Nobody knows what future holds
Until future, in reality, unfolds.

Pendulum's middle course of two extremes
An ideological equilibrium in life it seems,
Of measured optimum or a course of moderation,
Only a passing solution, can't stop defying motion.

Pendulum stops, motion stops,
Motion stops, life ends.
Life is motion,
Motion is life.

17.12.2013

PLANET EARTH

Time and motion in a wide infinite space,
Evidently, in a relentless forward race.
Earth's revolutions counting day and night,
Like a never ending eternal space flight—

All life, huddled together, by earth's gravity,
Ceaseless, endless motion through eternity.
Life, it seems, in constant process of evolution
Hand in hand with power of natural selection.

Adopting constantly with vagaries of environment,
Dynamic as nature does dictate and declare intent.
End result always is survival of the very fittest
And the strong finally seem to dominate the rest.

The sun, a powerhouse of inexhaustible energy,
Source of all life on earth and dictator of strategy,
In human mind, gave time a sense of dimension,
Captured in a clock for all human life to function.

Nature, it seems, is well able to balance
And stay well in course and in equilibrium,
Fear is, that relentless human interference,
Unwittingly, may stop nature's pendulum.

17.04.2012

PURE

Pure is the morning sunrise,
Holding in store, day's surprise!
Pure is a drop of morning dew,
Nature's way, cleansing anew.

Pure are the flowers, growing in the wild
And those in the garden we mind.
Pure is sweet smell of fragrant rose
Words fail description a poem or a prose.

Pure is water running down the mountain spring,
And echoes of sweet sound of birds singing.
Pure is music that touches all hearts
And creative emotions of all fine arts.

Pure is the lovers' very first tender kiss,
That ignites true love, an eternal bliss!
Pure is the heart that's always giving,
Love is gathered, hate is forgiving.

Pure is a newly born baby's mind
And love of mother and child that bind.
Pure is the taste of mother's cooking,
Fresh food and home baking.

Pure is truth and its utter simplicity,
Powers and preserves honesty and dignity.
Pure is knowledge and wisdom
An essence of enlightened kingdom.

11.11.2011

RAINBOW

I see a rainbow in the sky,
Colour splashed, standing high.
A beautiful archway,
To heaven's gateway.

Sunshine reflecting over
Clouds of rain,
Contrasting life of laughter
Over tears of pain.

Splashes of colours seen,
Violet, indigo, blue, green,
Yellow, orange and red;
All seven colours spectrum fed.

Hearts delight for all,
Men, women and children small.

01.12.2011

RELATIVE LIFE

Human cognition,
A process of relative deduction.

In darkness bring in light,
As daylight follow the night.

Pain's only measure,
If there is pleasure.

Only for bad, would
Good, really look good!

A friend to me
Is opposite to enemy.

Ugly is beauty's mother.
Without one, can't describe the other.

Hard to define male gender
Without female contender.

How can strong insist
If weak didn't exist?

The proud does best
In the company of modest.

We do need the small
To describe the tall.

Fast will get a blow,
If not faster than slow!

Love feels deep inside,
Beware! Hate is beside.

Winner takes all,
But, not if loser didn't fall!

Sandhurst 21.05.1984

SEVEN SENSES

For sight,
Nothing beats the morning light,
Sun promised ending every dark night,
A baby smiling in proud mother's arm,
Four seasons displaying own unique charm.

For sound,
Hear singing birds in the wild around,
Laughing children in the playground,
Sound of music played from the heart,
Lasting emotions of any performing art.

For smell,
A good spell—pick up a fragrant rose,
For a bad one—better close your nose,
Sweet smell of fresh food cooking,
Bread and cake in the oven baking.

For taste,
The baby claims, milk from mother's breast,
For some, 'tis mother's cooking at its best,
Fast food fans will, perhaps, disagree,
Then, many may claim they lack pedigree.

For touch,
Pleases much, when two hands shake befriended,
At times of need a helping hand extended,
The thrill and tenderness of lovers first kiss,
Life's incomplete if one's made to miss.

For security,
'Tis a priority, for fragile life's sanctity,
A marriage vow, a promise of fidelity,
A home, a shelter, a roof over our head,
A source of living, a supply of daily bread.

For love,
Standing above, all things emotional,
Love that's promised remains unconditional,
Mother's natural love for her child,
Fares well even in the wild.

24.05.2012

SPRING IS IN THE AIR

Sky is blue and turning fair,
Sensing Spring is in the air!
Leafy trees blowing sigh of relief
From bare boughs of Winter's grief,
Flowers begin to bud and bloom
Following Winter's chill and gloom.

Flowers first come into focus
Purple and white colour crocus
And delicate white snowdrops
Then, the daffodil's yellow crops
Smiling and waving in the mild sunshine
Beckoning the red tulips next in line.

A grand appearance from lifeless hours
By the big blossoms of magnolia flowers.
Bluebell's bustling bloom's speechless talks
Whisper in silent woodland walks.
Pretty primroses in posy postures
Peeping shyly in wild pastures.

Camellias in red white and pink,
Azaleas await April showers and blink,
Beautiful and full bloom in May,
Challenging cherry blossoms glory day.
May's flower show ablaze full on,
Here comes colour splashed rhododendron.

Migrating birds back in formation,
Animals ended their winter hibernation,
Robin redbreast busy building a nest,
Others' free enjoying Spring fest.
Wood pigeon, sparrow and bluetit I see
Along with blackbird, butterfly and busy bee.

Sun's Winter muffle is cast aside,
Floating clouds negotiating to hide,
The sun seeking to come out and play,
Staying longer and warmer each day,
Sensing an instinctive flair—
Spring is in the air!

09.05.2013

SUN SEASONS AND SENTIMENT

As the Summer sunshine slowly fades
And sheds gentle glow on Autumn shades,
Cool breeze caress falling leaves gently,
The sun still trying to kiss them warmly.

Birds, I believe, migrate to mild climate,
The rest get ready for Winter and hibernate.
For the young, hopes of Spring rising high,
But for the old, yet another year gone by.

Sandhurst 10.11.1984

THE CLOUD

I am transient in the endless sky,
I am the mere mortal's celestial eye,
Without my probity they are destined to die!
Who am I?

I am the mother of a few that render
Storm, rain, snow, hail, lightning and thunder.
I work hand in hand with the mighty sun
My work is never ending, but, it's fun!

Sun draws moisture from the seas and oceans,
Impregnates me with feminine emotions,
In agony I roar and thunder before water breaks,
Once over, in ecstasy, I sparkle in a form lightening takes.

With rain I fill the lakes as much as it takes,
Fresh water from heaven after the sun bakes,
I add life to the mountain springs and rills,
The rivers running through town and country fills.

I bring back flowers smiling after being parched,
I nourished the earth, that's no longer scorched,
I bring back the trees' colours bright and green,
Colours before my touch hadn't been seen.

Back above in the sky on my wing again, I float,
As I do, I watch and I spy and I take note,
If the sun becomes too strong for some to bear,
To provide shade where needed I begin to steer.

In the evening lull, if I feel playful and gay,
With silvery moon hide and seek I play
Beneath the stars far and near, twinkling,
Watching us play their eyes seem sparkling.

Once again, I float, I gloat, and I laugh loud in thunder,
I change attire many times, is that any wonder?
Amorous me, love to touch the mighty mountain peaks
And sweetly steel a kiss or two on my cheeks.

I see mortals bred, mortals fed, and mortals dead,
My celestial journey is eternal instead.
I am transient in the endless sky,
I am the mere mortal's celestial eye.

1.03.2013

THE SUN

The morning sun smiling, ushering a new day,
Waking the sleepy earth, a touch of pure potent ray,
Whispering hope and possibilities in new light,
Slowly, energising and negotiating, becoming bright.

Seeing a day's work over, setting in the far horizon west,
Colour and beauty inspire artists' and poets' imaginations'
best,
Sinking in profusion of colour under a luminous sky
With promise of another new day bids farewell and good
bye.

A gigantic sphere, a furnace of intense burning fire,
For generations, in awe, we humans look and admire
Sheer awe inspiring aesthetic beauty,
Relentless act of continuous creativity.

Wondrous eternal source of potent and vital energy,
Creating and sustaining life on earth and its ecology.
Rays of sunshine followed by reciprocal rain;
Essential ingredients help grow our daily grain.

A cauldron of incomprehensible atomic fusion,
A finely balanced course in space and motion.
A fractional deviation causing havoc and disruption
To weather pattern and life to function.

A defining factor of life, time, space and reasons
In moments, hours, days, months and seasons.

31.01.2012

TIME

To be alive is to sense the passage of time,
Can stop the clock but can't stop time.
Configuration of cognitive consciousness,
Time past, time present and time future sense.

Fundamentally motionless, not pure perception,
Reliant on relativity, space, matter and motion.
Impressionistic vocabulary
Of an experience sensory.

Cognitive consciousness conveys,
Audiovisual synchrony portrays
Past memory and present perception
Compile and constitute future conception.

Origin unfathomed, destination infinity,
Colourless, odourless, an eternal entity,
Silent and touch-insensitive, no height or breadth,
Void of all dimensions and depth.

Paradoxically, life's most prized and powerful phenomenon.
Never looks back, a dynamic forward force marching on.
Past never revisited—derelict, dead and demure.
History reveals footprints of time and tales of its tenure.

Life once thriving, failing and powerless at time's call.
Powerful, high and mighty, all submit and fall.
Wheel of time's eternal motion dominates this earth,
All life evolves from the beginning at birth.

Birth and baby's first cry announcing time's first call,
Death terminates, when the final curtains fall.
Generating new, budding, flowering, fruitful and furnished.
Degenerating to old, dated, neglected and tarnished.

Time—tenured, targeted and unmitigated.
Sun the energiser, source of all life created,
Gave time a dimension turning darkness into light,
Captured in a clock of twenty four hours day and night.

24.08.2012

TO BE OR NOT TO BE

To be brave,
Is not to kill but to save,
Treating life with utmost respect,
Live and let live, nothing's perfect.

To be powerful,
Is to channel the energy
Into something useful
For human cause and ecology.

To be honourable,
One must be able
To give honour to others where due,
Disagree, but able to respect others' view.

To hold high office,
Is not the ultimate prize,
Doubtless, it will entice
Higher and higher to rise.
'Tis a privilege and an opportunity,
To serve for the good of humanity.

To be charitable,
Is a deed most admirable,
But, giving for the sake of pity
Amounts to stealing dignity.
Discreet help securing a project
Preserves dignity not defeating the object.

To be rich,
Is to reach
Desired fulfilment
Happiness and contentment.

To be wise,
Is not to preach and advise,
But to live by example,
Seeking knowledge never is ample.

31.01.2012